I See My Consonant Teams

I See **TCH**

SHANNON ANDERSON

A Little Honey Book

Crabtree Publishing
crabtreebooks.com

I like to play
"I See."

Let's look and see what ends with **tch**.

I see a chick ha**tch**.

What do you see?

I see jeans with a pa**tch**.

What do you see?

I see kids pi**tch**
and ca**tch**.

What do you see?

I see a cat
take a stre**tch**.

What do you see?

I see a dog
scratch an itch.

What do you see?

What other words end with **tch**?

Do You See These?

batch	latch
butterscotch	match
crutch	sketch
fetch	stitch
hitch	stopwatch
hopscotch	watch
hutch	witch

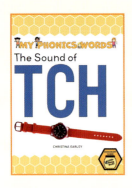

Read the nonfiction paired title *The Sound of TCH*.

I See TCH

Written by: Shannon Anderson
Designed by: Rhea Magaro
Series Development: James Earley
Editor: Kim Thompson
Educational Consultant: Marie Lemke M.Ed.

Illustrations: All images from Shutterstock: NotionPic: p. cover, 1, 2, 5, 7, 9, 11, 13, 14; Claudia M. Velasco: p. 4; SunshineVector: p. 4; Gurza: p. 5; Kovalova Marharyta: p. 6; Bibadash: p. 6; Viktorija Reuta: p. 7; Elyutina Polina: p. 7; BNP Design Studio: p. 8; ann_isme: p. 9; Pogorelova Olga: p. 9; Aigul V: p. 10; pikepicture: p. 10; Elena Pimukova: p. 11; vectorisland: p. 11; angkrit: p. 12; Nik Symkin: p. 13; Andrii Arkhipov: p. 14;

Crabtree Publishing

crabtreebooks.com   800-387-7650

Copyright © 2023 Crabtree Publishing

All rights reserved. No part of this publication may be reproduced, stored in a retrieval system or be transmitted in any form or by any means, electronic, mechanical, photocopying, recording, or otherwise, without the prior written permission of Crabtree Publishing.

Printed in the U.S.A./012023/
CG20220815

Published in Canada
Crabtree Publishing
616 Welland Ave.
St. Catharines, Ontario
L2M 5V6

Published in the United States
Crabtree Publishing
347 Fifth Ave
Suite 1402-145
New York, NY 10016

Library and Archives Canada Cataloguing in Publication
Available at Library and Archives Canada

Library of Congress Cataloging-in-Publication Data
Available at the Library of Congress

Hardcover: 978-1-0396-9624-2
Paperback: 978-1-0396-9731-7
Ebook (pdf): 978-1-0396-9945-8
Epub: 978-1-0396-9838-3